WRITING STARS

Edited By Iain McQueen

First published in Great Britain in 2022 by:

Young Writers
Remus House
Coltsfoot Drive
Peterborough
PE2 9BF
Telephone: 01733 890066
Website: www.youngwriters.co.uk

All Rights Reserved
Book Design by Ashley Janson
© Copyright Contributors 2021
Softback ISBN 978-1-80015-779-8

Printed and bound in the UK by BookPrintingUK
Website: www.bookprintinguk.com
YB0493M

FOREWORD

For Young Writers' latest competition This Is Me, we asked primary school pupils to look inside themselves, to think about what makes them unique, and then write a poem about it! They rose to the challenge magnificently and the result is this fantastic collection of poems in a variety of poetic styles.

Here at Young Writers our aim is to encourage creativity in children and to inspire a love of the written word, so it's great to get such an amazing response, with some absolutely fantastic poems. It's important for children to focus on and celebrate themselves and this competition allowed them to write freely and honestly, celebrating what makes them great, expressing their hopes and fears, or simply writing about their favourite things. This Is Me gave them the power of words. The result is a collection of inspirational and moving poems that also showcase their creativity and writing ability.

I'd like to congratulate all the young poets in this anthology, I hope this inspires them to continue with their creative writing.

CONTENTS

Aghadrumsee Primary School, Aghadrumsee

Chloe Mcvitty (10)	1
Erin McVitty (9)	2
Lewis Forster (9)	4
Jodie Robinson (10)	5
Sophie Morrison (10)	6
Ben Forster (10)	7
Megan McCauley (9)	8
Isaac Irwin (10)	9
Ellie McVitty (8)	10
Chloe Hall (11)	11
Abbie Coulson (10)	12
Amy McCauley (9)	13
Ollie Hall (8)	14
Ryan Mac Farlane (10)	15
George Doonan (8)	16
Scott Elliott (8)	17
Hannah Creighton-Clarke (9)	18

Barnes Farm Junior School, Chelmer Village

Emerson Tucker (7)	19
Emilia Blundell (7)	20
Amy Wheeler (7)	21
Gracie Mullem (8)	22
Krish MaheshNair (7)	23
Sophia Rolfe (7)	24
Rebecca Poole (7)	25
Olanna Gideon (8)	26
Teddy Witherick (7)	27
Zoe (7)	28
Joey Archer (7)	29
Kyle Parkhurst Sousa (8)	30
John Sharp (7)	31
Isla-Marie Davidson (7)	32
Sofia Mohammed (7)	33
Yiannis Karamitsios (7)	34
Sophia (7)	35
Samara Moledina (7)	36
Paola Tabegna (7)	37
Jodie Brewster (7)	38
Vanshika Bandaru (7)	39
Renée Williams (7)	40
Esosa Kanoba (8)	41
Lucy Welch (8)	42
Lacey Hawker-Jolly (7)	43
Saanvi Serene (7)	44
Ruby Ferraby-Wright (8)	45
Sisi Maneva (7)	46
Harvey Keane (7)	47
Amelia Williams (8)	48
Oliver Engwell (7)	49
Ada Parsons (7)	50
Olivia Boreham (7)	51
Leighton-Lei Chittock (7)	52
Archie Shape (7)	53
Oliver Price (8)	54
Thaleia Kougiami (7)	55
Jaeden Enver (7)	56
Indiana Rose Charles (8)	57
Mia Narayanaswamy (7)	58
Sophia Velichkova (7)	59
Sam Edwards (7)	60
Isla Hubble (8)	61
Annalise Leonard (7)	62
Ronnie Hopson (7)	63
Elsie Gibbons (7)	64
Poppy May Idzior (7)	65

Ibstock Place School, Roehampton

Amelie Clements (10)	66
Penelope Maurides (10)	68
Daisy Phillips (9)	70
Theo Collins (10)	72
William Richardson (8)	74
Jack Barrigan (10)	76
Emily Sermon (8)	78
Raffy Youle (9)	80
Imogen Beattie (9)	82
Vicente Buyo (8)	84
Ena Zhang (11)	86
Aurora Hanlon (9)	88
Rafi Brenninkmeijer (9)	90
Grace McTaggart (8)	91
Tory Song (10)	92
Emma Kovalchuk (10)	94
William Rettie (10)	96
Kit Kroft (10)	98
Imogen Kilshaw (8)	100
Emmeline Anderson (10)	102
Gabriella Lumley (8)	104
Aria Kathuria (9)	105
Scarlett Levy (8)	106
Milly Carter (8)	107
Nikolai Jönsson (8)	108
Isaac Anand (9)	110
Gabriella Lumley	112
Holly Flowers (11)	113
Lukas Lau (10)	114
Athena Karamanou (10)	115
Meher Sethi (8)	116
Yinuo Pu (10)	117
Fenella Houlihan (11)	118
Alessia Fantuzzi (8)	119
Trephena Glanville (10)	120
Isla Roberts (9)	121
Eric Zeng (10)	122
Maria Steier (10)	123
Alessandro	124
Ella Schoelzel Sipahi (10)	125
Maya Peters (9)	126
Jake Ballantyne (9)	127
Gaspar Velasco (11)	128
Noah Beattie (8)	129
Kiran Mahan (10)	130
Anoushka Green (9)	131
Francisco Daganski-Evans (9)	132
Thomas Petrou (10)	133
Ella Smith (9)	134
Hanna Ghods (8)	135
Paloma Gwyer (10)	136
Sophia Cho (8)	137
Maria Isabel Buyo (10)	138
William Lambert (10)	139
Isobel Dajani (9)	140
Denis Rodionov (9)	141
Poppy Letting (10)	142
Eudora Wawra (8)	143
Sibylla Coleman (11)	144
Noah Streule (9)	145
Katerina Godunova (9)	146
Hollie Hughes (9)	147
Sam Hilsley (10)	148
Freya Bittan (9)	149
Evangeline Sochovsky (10)	150
Izzy Houlihan (9)	151
Rosetta Weng (9)	152
Robyn Taskis (10)	153
Andreas Anagnostopulos (9)	154
Owen Herpers (10)	155
Federico Cortinovis (9)	156
Rafe Bolger (8)	157
Oscar Homerstone (10)	158
Dylan Phillips (10)	159
Ryan Choi (10)	160
Ali Charchafchi (11)	161
Henry O'Donnell (10)	162
Maren-Amelie Kilshaw (10)	163
Arion-Derin Paparizos (8)	164
Hasan Al-Khatib	165
Leonardo Di Dio (8)	166
Jenson Boyd (9)	167
Jing Tong Lyu (9)	168
Aurelia O'Connor Lally (8)	169

Andrey Varilow	170
Pedro Henrique Stuckert Weber Dos Santos (8)	171
Lina Tikriti (10)	172
Hanna Kivinen (10)	173
Michaela Tsapralis (10)	174
Mason Elwin-Davis (10)	175
Sonya Kunts (10)	176
William Cook (9)	177
Leo Hellier (10)	178
Huxley Coombes (9)	179
Arthur Tilev-Maroney (8)	180
Rupert le Roux (9)	181
Christopher-John Martin (10)	182
Elmar Streule (7)	183
Isabella Coombes (11)	184
Gabriella Blundell (9)	185
Kaan Ulgen (10)	186
Erin Donovan (7)	187
Benjamin Whitby-Smith (7)	188
Cynthia (Xinyue) Zhang (7)	189
Xanthe Michael (7)	190
Lucas Quin (8)	191
Max Harrison (9)	192
Delfina Vocos Aguirre (7)	193
Grayston Conroy (7)	194
Alessandro Jacob Shamim (7)	195
Hugh Smith (11)	196
Celina Poshkus (7)	197
Carine Levy (7)	198
Felix George O'Donnell (7)	199
Isabella Zavos (7)	200
Benjamin Vocus (7)	201
Felix Currie (7)	202
Ellie Howarth-Saunders (7)	203
Isla Pollock (7)	204
Naba Hasmi (7)	205
Sophia Dell (7)	206
Harper Tricker (7)	207
Alice Leonard (7)	208
Luka Taborin (8)	209
Hari Haddock (7)	210
Hugo le Roux (7)	211

Pool Hayes Primary School, Willenhall

Saffron Banga (11)	212
Gia Halpin	215
Ruby Hewitt (11)	216
Maddison-Leigh Brittle (10)	218
Ghianna Jean Parry	219

Wakefield Methodist Junior & Infant School, Thornes

Zakariya Ali (11)	220
Lilac Sherwood (10)	221
Isobel Cook (10)	222
Eliza Dorothy Hodgkins (10)	223
Matilda Baker (10)	224
Ava Mellor (10)	225
William Barnsley (10)	226
Mac Copley (10)	227
Ava Mae Dean Blades (10)	228
Mohammed Aslam (10)	229
Tommy Bramley (10)	230
C T Robinson-Rowe (10)	231
Kasim Ramzan (10)	232
Jessica Greer (10)	233
Noah Christopher David Egan (10)	234
Ali Sharif (10)	235
Dexter Oakland (10)	236
Nathan Williams (10)	237
Daud Rehman (10)	238
Tien Tattersall (10)	239
Dylan Smith (10)	240

THE POEMS

This Is Me

I am a great gangster gamer
I love cricket with my big, bad bat
I am a chef in my chef hat and apron
My paintings are as good as Van Gogh's
My baby sister is Leah, she is as cheeky as a monkey
I can be helpful looking after cheeky monkey Leah

My calf Bella Blue is as wild as a free reign horse
Buster and Sooty are my cats
And they catch thousands of rats
I have two chickens called Pepper and Salt
And their names a probably insults
My favourite animal would be a pink paradise pig

I laugh like a hyena when somebody cracks me up
I am as tall as a giraffe you could say
My hair has Goldilocks' streaks
My eyes are green peas
This is me!

Chloe Mcvitty (10)
Aghadrumsee Primary School, Aghadrumsee

This Is Me

I am a lightning bolt
On the football field
Faster than a cat
I run as soon as I see a wasp

I really love to read
But one thing
I love more
Than reading is
Art
I'm as arty as a paint palette

My hair is golden in the sun
But when it's dull
My hair is as red as a rose
My eyes shine like
Green pearls

In class, I count
Down the seconds until maths
Because I love it
Unlike literacy

I have lots of friends
At our houses we eat sweets
And chocolate
While we talk

This is me!

Erin McVitty (9)
Aghadrumsee Primary School, Aghadrumsee

This Is Me

I am as good a gamer as T-Fue
I am a thumbs-on-fire kid
I'm not a fan of Adopt Me
I have great gaming skills
Though I like to read a lot too

I have lots of cool pets
Morris, Shadow and Muffin
Television is my dogs' favourite noise
I love them very much
Even with all their crazy sounds

I always really enjoy my food
Pizza, burgers and roast dinner too
These are my favourite foods to eat
And I like to drink Fanta as a treat

So all I think about is
Gaming, reading, food and all my pets
This is me.

Lewis Forster (9)
Aghadrumsee Primary School, Aghadrumsee

I Am Unique

My skin is as pink as a peach
My eyes are as brown as hazelnuts
My hair is like chocolate mousse
My voice is like an angel, well so I think
I'm a cheetah reading
And a dolphin in the water
I have extremely crazy friends who are loads of fun
I'm as bright as the sun
My favourite thing to bake is buns
I'm really fun but some days I can be glum
My friends say I'm as delightful as a dolphin
I'm a Liverpool supporter at heart
Maths is an orange traffic light for me
But I try my best, no matter what it may be.

Jodie Robinson (10)
Aghadrumsee Primary School, Aghadrumsee

This Is Me

I am as tall as a giant giraffe
I can see the clouds with my long neck
I love my pet dog Tiny
Tiny is very tiny, aged forty-one
She has a big bark for a tiny dog
A Jack Russell

I am as amazing as an avocado
That's what my friends say
Even though I don't like fruit
My hair is brown like chocolate
The colour of my eyes are blue, just like my family
Even Tiny has blue eyes
I am as clever as a teacher
Sometimes and sometimes not
This is me!

Sophie Morrison (10)
Aghadrumsee Primary School, Aghadrumsee

I Am

I am as mini as a mouse
Hiding in his home
Having a nap in my bed

I am as smart as a snake
Slithering through a maths book
Waiting for the next calculation

I am as fast as a cheetah
Running down the football pitch
My football boots on fire

I am as brave as a lion
Roaring through the land
Eating his dinner in the sun

I am as hardworking as a wolf
Keeping watch on my den
Sticking close to my lunatic friends.

Ben Forster (10)
Aghadrumsee Primary School, Aghadrumsee

This Is Me

I am as sweet as a cherry,
I am very kind and caring,
I'm always helping,
My talent is skipping,
My favourite pet is my dog,
He likes playing with me,
My eyes are like my mummy's jewellery,
My hair is as long as a giraffe's neck,
I love my teddies because they're soft,
I am as organised as a receptionist,
I love chatting like a cheeky monkey,
This is me!

Megan McCauley (9)
Aghadrumsee Primary School, Aghadrumsee

This Is Me

T he thing that makes me, me, is my love for animals
H ugs are my speciality
I love Red Panda's food, it's my favourite
S ometimes I like to sleep in

I love Spudnick, he is my favourite cow
S chool is a nice place to be

M y favourite thing to do is go to my aunt's house
E ach day is a new adventure for me.

Isaac Irwin (10)
Aghadrumsee Primary School, Aghadrumsee

This Is Me

T ennis is my hobby
H ustling in football is what I do
I love my family including my dog and my cat
S inging is my favourite thing to do

I love to dance and I am really good at it
S kittles are my favourite thing to eat

M y best friends are always there for me
E yes are brown like biscuits, my hair is a red rose.

Ellie McVitty (8)
Aghadrumsee Primary School, Aghadrumsee

This Is Me

I am as clever as a calculator
Math is my best subject so I am told
I am as fast as a cheetah
I am as calm as a calf
My eyes are blue footballs
Like fireworks dancing in the dark sky
My friends are lunatics
But my best friend is Bono my dog
My hair is golden blonde
Like sand on the beach
I love to play football
I am like sonic in my boots
This is me!

Chloe Hall (11)
Aghadrumsee Primary School, Aghadrumsee

This Is Me

I am as sweet as a strawberry
I am as special as a diamond, so I am told
I am a cheetah on rollerskates
I am as sunny as the sun
My heart is as big as the world
My eyes are big, brown marbles
My favourite thing to do is to have cuddles with Coco my cat
Math, spiders and the dark give me the shivers
I love all animals, red pandas are my favourite
This is me!

Abbie Coulson (10)
Aghadrumsee Primary School, Aghadrumsee

I Am Me

I am as sporty as Ronaldo
I am as clever as a high school student
I am as fast as a cheetah
My hair is long like a stripe of sand
In class I count down the seconds to hometime
I am a family person
My eyes are blue like the Atlantic Ocean
I'm a Manchester United supporter
I enjoy farming with my dad
I love school because I get to see my friends.

Amy McCauley (9)
Aghadrumsee Primary School, Aghadrumsee

This Is Me

I like rugby, I train with Daddy lifting weights
I am as fast as a supercar
I love laughing with my friends
I love it when the bell rings for a snack
I love snack time
I am as fit as a fiddle
I love going on my go-kart and my bike
I would love to be a famous rugby player
I love going into the greenhouse and seeing all the plants.

Ollie Hall (8)
Aghadrumsee Primary School, Aghadrumsee

This Is Me

I'm as fast as a cheetah
I'm as happy as a hyena
I'm as funny as a monkey
I'm as fierce as a fox
I'm as kind as a cat
I'm so fast just like my two dogs
I'm as angry as a gorilla
I'm as bright as the blazing sun
I'm as silly as a goat
This is me.

Ryan Mac Farlane (10)
Aghadrumsee Primary School, Aghadrumsee

This Is Me

I am as fast as a sugar rush,
My eyes are as blue as the sky,
I climb like I am a gorilla,
My body is a wiggly, wobbly gummy worm,
I am as smart as a walking computer,
My mouth is always zipped up,
I am as bright as a star,
My favourite thing in school is maths,
This is me.

George Doonan (8)
Aghadrumsee Primary School, Aghadrumsee

This Is Me

I climb like a monkey
My eyes are like blue footballs
I am a farming man, it's in my blood
I love sweets
One day I am going to turn into one
I am as crazy as a gorilla
I am as silly as six sausages
I am as fit as a farmer
I am as fast as a Lamborghini
This is me.

Scott Elliott (8)
Aghadrumsee Primary School, Aghadrumsee

This Is Me

T wo playful pet cats
H appy and cheerful
I am kind and caring
S uper at art

I love my family
S uper at baking

M y favourite game is Roblox
E njoy golden time and eating pizza.

Hannah Creighton-Clarke (9)
Aghadrumsee Primary School, Aghadrumsee

This Is Me

I am a superstar
I am an awesome athlete
I am a football lover
I am a fabulous footballer player
I am as fast as a lightning bolt
I am a hero when it comes to helping people
My hair is as blonde as the sand
I am as sporty as a mouse
My favourite desserts are brownies and red velvet cake
I am very good at English
I am very friendly
My tiny dog is called Bo and she has brown fur
My dog is a half pug and half Jack Russell
My favourite dinners are burgers and homemade pizza
I am very helpful
This is me.

Emerson Tucker (7)
Barnes Farm Junior School, Chelmer Village

This Is Me

I am as kind as a ladybird
I am as gentle as a dog
I am as helpful as a teacher
I am generous
I am loving like a horse
I am thoughtful
I am weird like my bestie
I like cake
I love animals
I am a lover of gymnastics
I am as creative as my favourite art YouTuber Zach
My eyes are like the blue sea
My hair is as brown as coconut shells
This is me.

Emilia Blundell (7)
Barnes Farm Junior School, Chelmer Village

This Is Me

T his is all about me
H i I am an active girl
I ce cream is the best food, inside my brain is really fun
S aturday is one of the best days

I am the best
S aturdays and Sundays I wake up at 8 o'clock

M onday is my packed lunch day
E very day we are at school I wake up at 7 o'clock.

Amy Wheeler (7)
Barnes Farm Junior School, Chelmer Village

This Is Me

I am a beautiful ballerina
Gentle on my toes
I am a skater, skimming across the gym floor
I am a happy hairstyler with snippy fingers
I am a positive person like a unicorn
My smile is as shiny as the seaside
My hair is as simple as a shop
My eyes are as green as a garden bush
My legs are as thick as a tube
My nails are as white as a wall.

Gracie Mullem (8)
Barnes Farm Junior School, Chelmer Village

This Is Me

I am good at football
I am as kind as God
I am as fast as a lightning bolt
I am as stealthy as a ninja
I am a big fan of Pokémon
I am a huge fan of McDonald's
I am as brave as a superhero
I am a fan of playing video games
I am as sneaky as a cat
I am as creative as an engineer
I am as helpful as a doctor
This is me.

Krish MaheshNair (7)
Barnes Farm Junior School, Chelmer Village

This Is Me

I am a lover of animals
I like reading big books
I am very good at dancing
I am very good at singing
I like going to the park
I like playing with my brother
I have blonde hair
I have green eyes
I love hot chocolate
I love seeing my friends
I like going on a walk
I like swimming
I like riding my bike
This is me.

Sophia Rolfe (7)
Barnes Farm Junior School, Chelmer Village

This Is Me

T he ice cream man I love
H olidays are the best
I love looking at spiders, but my mum doesn't
S uperstar singer

I am as loving as a baby panda
S ometimes I am a good dancer, sometimes I am not

M y friends are Olana and Emilia
E nd of this is now.

Rebecca Poole (7)
Barnes Farm Junior School, Chelmer Village

This Is Me

T all in size and as tall as a giraffe
H air in hundreds of plaits
I ce cream lover
S aturday is my favourite day of the week

I have chocolate-brown eyes
S ee me do a lot of cartwheels

M y favourite colour is a dark indigo
E ven as fast as a cheetah.

Olanna Gideon (8)
Barnes Farm Junior School, Chelmer Village

This Is Me

T his is all about me
H e loves PE
I love making cakes
S trong as a snake

I can cook like a chef
S pecial book reader and my favourite is called Beth

M inecraft is my favourite game
E verything here is all about me, and actually, I am pretty plain.

Teddy Witherick (7)
Barnes Farm Junior School, Chelmer Village

This Is Me

T iny in size
H ave a lot of interesting books
I love cold ice cream
S easide is as sandy as a sandpit

I love pets, they run so quickly
S ometimes I get to wake my dog

M y books are as interesting as a butterfly
E lephants are okay.

Zoe (7)
Barnes Farm Junior School, Chelmer Village

This Is Me

I am a lightning bolt in races
I am a superstar speeder at running
I am good at helping my family out
I am good at flips on my trampoline
I am a super Sonic fan
I can run past you in a flash
I am good at using the colours of the rainbow
To do perfect painting
This is me.

Joey Archer (7)
Barnes Farm Junior School, Chelmer Village

This Is Me

I am a brave lion
I am a fantastic friend
Always there to lend a hand
I am a lightning bolt
With football boots that strike
I am a monkey, always crazy and cheeky
My eyes are like chocolate buttons
My legs are tall and thin like a giraffe
My pencil is as sharp as a pin.

Kyle Parkhurst Sousa (8)
Barnes Farm Junior School, Chelmer Village

This Is Me

T his is all about me
H i I am an art ninja
I love painting
S uper Stone Age man

I am as funny as a clown
S unshine is my favourite weather

M y dad is a bit sporty
E very day I wake up at 7 o'clock.

John Sharp (7)
Barnes Farm Junior School, Chelmer Village

This Is Me

T he best
H oola hooper
I love zebras and giraffes
S nakes are creepy

I do not like spiders
S ometimes I'm as creative as an artist

M ummy is the best
E lephants are big and I've fed one too.

Isla-Marie Davidson (7)
Barnes Farm Junior School, Chelmer Village

This Is Me

I am a great gymnast, stretchy as an elastic band
I am the sun, bold and shining bright
I am like a spiralled jaguar, roaring free but always ready to pounce
My eyes are chocolate saucers
My smile is as wide as the Cheshire Cat's
Huge from ear to ear
This is me.

Sofia Mohammed (7)
Barnes Farm Junior School, Chelmer Village

This Is Me

T all in size
H ave no sisters
I love ice cream
S aturdays are my favourite day

I love dogs
S ometimes he barks though

M y eyes are green like grass
E lephants are large like my dad.

Yiannis Karamitsios (7)
Barnes Farm Junior School, Chelmer Village

This Is Me

I am a cheetah, fast and quiet
My hair is like a bear, smooth and brown
I am a nurse, kind and helpful
My eyes are chocolate bourbons yummy
I am a crab, silly and clumsy
I am a dog, playful and happy
My teeth are white shiny ribbons
This is me!

Sophia (7)
Barnes Farm Junior School, Chelmer Village

This Is Me

I'm a graceful and good gymnast
Like a flamingo
I am a good friend
Like a cute dog and its puppy
I am a good listener
Like a bat with good hearing
My hair is as straight as glass
My eyes are like chocolate buttons
This is me.

Samara Moledina (7)
Barnes Farm Junior School, Chelmer Village

This Is Me

I am a beautiful ballerina, gentle on my toes
I am a superstar singer, my voice is so loud that everyone can hear
I'm fast and fresh like a cheetah that everyone can see
I am as funny as a clown, everyone laughs
My eyes are like brown chocolate.

Paola Tabegna (7)
Barnes Farm Junior School, Chelmer Village

This Is Me

I am a hedgehog, helpful and happy
I am a kangaroo, kind and keeping my joey safe
I am a respectful rabbit
With long ears pricked, standing tall always
My hair is as blonde as a golden mane
My glasses are purple plums
This is me.

Jodie Brewster (7)
Barnes Farm Junior School, Chelmer Village

This Is Me

I'm a lover of gymnastics
I can do a one-handed cartwheel
My eyes are as black as coal
And I am kind as a rabbit
My favourite colour is blue and I love to read
I like drawing and I love to sing
I love myself
This is me.

Vanshika Bandaru (7)
Barnes Farm Junior School, Chelmer Village

This Is Me

I am a brilliant ballerina
Gentle on my toes
I am an elephant, always listening to you
I am homely, safe and sound
Like a hedgehog hibernating
My personality is as sharp as a tiger
My eyes are green globes
This is me.

Renée Williams (7)
Barnes Farm Junior School, Chelmer Village

This Is Me

I am a talking toad but I can't jump
I am a magical mathematician
Wishing away maths problems
I am a peaceful puppy
As soft as a pillow
My hair is as black as coal
My shoulders are as stiff as a rock
This is me.

Esosa Kanoba (8)
Barnes Farm Junior School, Chelmer Village

This Is Me

I am a lazy cat, that doesn't want to wake from their sleep
I am a beautiful ballerina, light on my toes
I am a superstar skipper, why isn't that my name
My hair is an outrageous orange
My eyes are oceans deep and blue.

Lucy Welch (8)
Barnes Farm Junior School, Chelmer Village

This Is Me

T his is all about me
H amsters are my favourite pet
I am as beautiful as a butterfly
S now days are the best

M y favourite things are butterflies
E very day I go to gymnastics.

Lacey Hawker-Jolly (7)
Barnes Farm Junior School, Chelmer Village

This Is Me

I am a pianist, peaceful
And particular
I am a mischievous monkey
Cheeky and sneaky
My hair is a calm sea without the waves
My face lights up
Like a star
I am as graceful as a swan
This is me.

Saanvi Serene (7)
Barnes Farm Junior School, Chelmer Village

This Is Me

I am as helpful as my mum
I am a superstar dancer
I am cheesy like pizza
I am as sporty as a footballer
I am an excellent singer
My hair is as brown as chocolate
My eyes are as brown as a coconut shell.

Ruby Ferraby-Wright (8)
Barnes Farm Junior School, Chelmer Village

This Is Me

I am a descriptive dancer, up on my toes
I am a secret squirrel, scattering all the acorns
I am a hopeful hairdresser
My eyes are brown like chocolate buttons
My hair is brown like gravy sauce.
This is me!

Sisi Maneva (7)
Barnes Farm Junior School, Chelmer Village

This Is Me

I am a dolphin in the water, fast and diving high
I am a clumsy crab, hard as steel
I am a peacock, polite and proud
I am a king, kind and handsome
My eyes are blue blueberries
My face shines like the sun.

Harvey Keane (7)
Barnes Farm Junior School, Chelmer Village

This Is Me

I am a messy mouse
Swinging across the floor
I am a fantastic footballer
I am a fab friend
Always a lending ear
My skin is as white as a ghost
My eyes are as blue as a blueberry
This is me.

Amelia Williams (8)
Barnes Farm Junior School, Chelmer Village

This Is Me

I am a super striker, feet like lightning
I as fast as a secret squirrel
I am a crocodile in the water, snappy and drippy
My hair is as golden as the sun
My eyes are like chocolate buttons.

Oliver Engwell (7)
Barnes Farm Junior School, Chelmer Village

This Is Me

I am a football lover
I love my family especially my sister
I love cats and dogs and bunnies
I can eat lots of ice cream
My hair is golden like the sun
My eyes are as green as grass.

Ada Parsons (7)
Barnes Farm Junior School, Chelmer Village

This Is Me

I am a really good friend
I am an excellent dancer
I love all animals
I can eat lots of ice cream
I am as creative as an artist
My hair is as blonde as sand
This is me.

Olivia Boreham (7)
Barnes Farm Junior School, Chelmer Village

This Is Me

I am a great ninja
I am a great runner
I am a great Pokémon Go player
I am a great lucky Leighton
I am a super racer
I am a super writer
I am a great helper.

Leighton-Lei Chittock (7)
Barnes Farm Junior School, Chelmer Village

This Is Me

I am a superstar singer
I am fun
Everyone's brains explode
I am so well behaved
My teeth are as sharp as a gorilla's
My ears are like bats'
This is me.

Archie Shape (7)
Barnes Farm Junior School, Chelmer Village

This Is Me

My eyes are as blue as the sky
My brown hair is like a grizzly bear
I am as tall as a tower
I am a fantastic friend
I am as hungry as a hyena
This is me.

Oliver Price (8)
Barnes Farm Junior School, Chelmer Village

This Is Me

I am a detailed drawer
My hair is shiny silk
I am caring, kind and confident
My eyes are dark brown like chocolate
And I am a super-duper swimmer
This is me.

Thaleia Kougiami (7)
Barnes Farm Junior School, Chelmer Village

This Is Me

I am as creative as the moon
I am as sneaky as a ninja
I am a whale and dinosaur fan
I am a superstar hooper
My eyes are as green as a swamp
This is me!

Jaeden Enver (7)
Barnes Farm Junior School, Chelmer Village

This Is Me

I'm a superstar singer
My hair is as wavy as the sea
I'm a flexible fantastic gymnast
I am a creative crafter
I am a crazy chatter
This is me.

Indiana Rose Charles (8)
Barnes Farm Junior School, Chelmer Village

This Is Me

I am a sensational sewer
My eyes are like storms in the night sky
My hair is as chilly as a Curly Wurly
I am fantastic at gymnastics
I am a divine dancer.

Mia Narayanaswamy (7)
Barnes Farm Junior School, Chelmer Village

This Is Me

I am a super swimmer
My eyes are green gems
My hair is as soft as a feather
My skin is as smooth as a piece of paper
I am as happy as a dog playing fetch.

Sophia Velichkova (7)
Barnes Farm Junior School, Chelmer Village

This Is Me

I am as fast as lightning
My hair is as soft as silk
My eyes are as green as emeralds
I am a fantastic friend
I am a shoulder to cry on
This is me.

Sam Edwards (7)
Barnes Farm Junior School, Chelmer Village

This Is Me

I am a great gymnast
My hair is as thick as a fluffy cheetah
I am a shoulder to cry on
My eyes are chocolate
I am a fantastic friend
This is me.

Isla Hubble (8)
Barnes Farm Junior School, Chelmer Village

This Is Me

I am a superstar swimmer
My hair is as soft as a scarf
I am a really confident reader
My eyes are as blue as the sea
I am a happy horse rider.

Annalise Leonard (7)
Barnes Farm Junior School, Chelmer Village

This Is Me

My eyes are blue like the ocean
My hair is as blonde as the beach
I am a great football player
I am a terrific friend
I am as strong as an ox.

Ronnie Hopson (7)
Barnes Farm Junior School, Chelmer Village

This Is Me

My eyes are brown like chocolate
I am good at gymnastics
I am a sensational singer
I am a fantastic friend
My eyes are brown chestnuts.

Elsie Gibbons (7)
Barnes Farm Junior School, Chelmer Village

This Is Me

My eyes are shining emeralds
I am a creative cook
My hair is as wavy as the ocean
I am a fantastic friend
I am a kind and loving soul.

Poppy May Idzior (7)
Barnes Farm Junior School, Chelmer Village

This Is Me

This is me, Amelie Clements
I am a daughter, niece, sister, granddaughter and friend
One thing is certain, on me you can always depend

This is me, gleeful and happy all the time
With a smile on my face to cheer you up when you are down
I will get rid of your frown

This is me, dance and drama are my things
Playing the violin and singing too
I'm always keen to try something new

This is me, I might not be good at climbing or heights
But I am decent at giving things a go
To cheat or lie that is not me
I would never stoop so low

This is me, if I get something wrong, then I get back up
I try and try again, always trying my best whatever the task
Whatever the outcome, whether I come first or last

This is me when you need a friend, I'm always there
Giving support, helping with jobs or telling jokes
In return, my friends help me when I am stuck, they are my folks

This is me, Amelie Clements
I don't care what anyone else thinks
Clements never give up, this motto to a Clements always links.

Amelie Clements (10)
Ibstock Place School, Roehampton

All About Me

I am a passionate climber,
An eager learner,
I am caring and sympathetic,
Wild and energetic,
My friends consider me loyal,
I am shy and go into a tight coil,
I am as hard-working as a bee,
Polite, optimistic, vibrant, that's me!

I adore taking my dog for walks
I could do it for hours.
I am a joyful butterfly, fluttering through gorgeous flowers.
My fingers dance on the piano while I'm music-making
I adore the sweet scent of crunchy cookies baking.

I am funny and friendly,
Thoughtful and trustworthy,
I am mature and respectful,
Kind and helpful,
I like climbing trees and am adventurous

Occasionally curious,
I am creative and lively,
I usually reply honestly,

Now this poem must be ceased,
Resilience, smartness, courage, determination are some of my qualities that can't be decreased.

Penelope Maurides (10)
Ibstock Place School, Roehampton

This Is Daisy

To create me you will need:

A bit of grump, hoodies and shorts
A pinch of laziness and sleeping in bed
Fifty grams of guitar music
A dash of paint and art
100 grams of animals
A tablespoon of weekend gaming
A sprinkle of family, fidgets and stationery
A bit of gymnastics in the garden

First, add 100 grams of whisked animals
Next, add a sprinkle of fun, family, fidgets and stationery
For a creative Daisy, add a dash of paint and art
Don't tell anyone, but a pinch of laziness and sleep in bed
A tablespoon of weekend gaming
Next, a load of cartwheeling in the garden
Add some hoodies and shorts
A whisk of grump and anger that I use
Next, mix thoroughly and pour into a tin

Place me in the oven but do not overbake
This could cause more grump than needed
This is me!

Daisy Phillips (9)
Ibstock Place School, Roehampton

Theo Collins

My name is Theo,
I like rugby,
I think you can see,
I'm not a bee,
I'm as small as a pea,
But that doesn't matter, it's me,
When I sing a song I feel like Donkey Kong,
My life is long,
I played rugby and hurt my knee,
Where I found a key,
For free cuddles,
I love my family,
Even when they make me do homework,
I play in the garden,
With my brother,
He is so nice, he's like my mother,
Who I smother in baby cream,
Then she starts to scream,
And I turn green,
It's very mean,

And my dad,
Is very rad,
Definitely not bad,
My sister,
is very nice,
Her skin is as cold as ice,
And as stretchy as mine,
I got a new rugby ball,
It's very cool,
South Africa did a maul,
This is me!

Theo Collins (10)
Ibstock Place School, Roehampton

This Is Me

My name is William
I love vehicles and especially cars
I like to watch videos about luxury yachts
As well as playing with my fantastic friends
I like making secret dens and extreme forts
That you have to see
I also love playing exciting football
I can ride a bike as fast as a supercar
I also am as lame as a cow
But I also love to make music with drums at my house
But nobody likes but I like it
Also Harry Potter is my favourite book
I think my look is pretty good
Also my sister said I'm annoying
But it's not true
But I am very boring
But the truth is she is annoying
My sister also throws things at me
But I don't care

I think I've finished and then she says
No, you're not and she gets angry!

William Richardson (8)
Ibstock Place School, Roehampton

Who Am I?

I am caring and kind,
With a creative mind,
I am an amazing friend,
If you're in trouble, my hand I will lend.

I am playful and fun,
A proud son,
A star flying free,
There is only one me!

I try to make others giggle,
I dance, slide and wiggle,
I'm like a clown,
I'll help when your spirits are down!

I play football every day,
It makes my cares float away,
I really like food,
It lifts my mood!

I'm not the brightest bulb in the store,
But I try my best and sometimes I fail,
And I know my friends are there for me,
To cheer me up and make me happy.

In short,
No one is perfect, everyone's unique,
And to answer the question,
I am whoever I want to be.

Jack Barrigan (10)
Ibstock Place School, Roehampton

A Rhyming Poem About Me

I like the colour orange, I think it's swell
I like the colour yellow as well
I don't like the colour pink
I think it stinks
My hair and eyes are brown
I don't live in the country, I live in the town
I chew my hair which is bad, so I have been told
Sometimes when people are warm I am cold
My favourite animal is a dog
I like to walk on logs
In prep three we've done a very cringey song called the midnight tango
I hate the fruit dried mango
Being creative is my superpower
Geography makes me cower
I'm as slow as a sloth
I also like moths
I like things that are sour
I haven't but I want to climb the Eiffel Tower

I wish I could use a made-up word like moem
Always that's the poem.

Emily Sermon (8)
Ibstock Place School, Roehampton

This Is Me

This is what you need to create me:

15 kilograms of fantastic sportsmanship
30 grams of competitivity
6 kilograms of sugar
9 kilograms of speed
5 kilograms of stamina
59 kilograms of amazing at football
70 grams of happiness
90 grams of funniness
50 grams of wonderful limbing
80 grams of adventuring
30 grams of skilful pool playing
90 more grams of swimming
10 grams of superb baking
20 grams of rage
90 grams of creativity
90 grams of reading
80 grams of tasty chips
2kg of smiling

Now mix thoroughly
Put on a baking tray
Now put in a piping hot oven
Take it out of the oven
Now put it in the pan flip it in the air so it lands perfectly
Bon appetit
Who wants to eat?

Raffy Youle (9)
Ibstock Place School, Roehampton

A Recipe For Me

A dollop of dog-loving powder
A pinch of creativeness
Two spoonfuls of sugar
Lots of chocolate
A handful of creativeness
A big chunk of energy
A bunch of friends
A fast-thinking, creative mind
Some butter
Two paintbrushes

In a bowl, pour in the chocolate, sugar and energy gently
Stir over a low heat to make a thick paste to produce the need for speed
Add the dog-loving powder, uniqueness and butter
Pop in the microwave for thirty seconds, this will make kindness
Add the paintbrushes and very gently stir to make a masterpiece
Mix the rest of the ingredients in a separate bowl

Then add a pinch of salt and pour in both mixtures
then put it in the oven for fifteen minutes
To make me!

Imogen Beattie (9)
Ibstock Place School, Roehampton

The Recipe That Makes Me

You will need:

A handful of sport
A pinch of sugar
A lot of love
A teaspoon of maths
A big bit of caring
a tiny bit of tea
A lot of speed
Mischief and fun
And caramel icing

First of all, you need three kilograms of love and then add one kilogram of caring
Then mix it well
A teaspoon of maths should be next put in
Then a big fat grin
A pinch of sugar for some sweet taste
A handful of sports
Now add a bit of tea
Mix it thoroughly

Put in three kilograms of speed as fast as a cheetah
One kilogram of mischief and fun
Put it in the oven until it is golden brown
Then put caramel icing
Put it in the freezer for about three minutes
Bon appetit.

Vicente Buyo (8)
Ibstock Place School, Roehampton

This Is Me

I am a passionate dancer
Who is still a learner
And when I'm on point
I do not worry that I'll disappoint

I am a hard-working bee
And I like to believe
I am the oldest girl in the year
And turning eleven was no fear

When I started year six
It was a very weird mix
But I'm sure ill have no problem
And will always reach my maximum

I've been in school for seven straight years
And it's time to wipe up my tears
I am always going to be strong
Whenever I am wrong

Even though I'm quiet as a mouse and shy as a butterfly
I'm sure I'll be brave enough just to say hi
Now you've read about me
I hope I can go down in history!

Ena Zhang (11)
Ibstock Place School, Roehampton

Recipe For Me

To create me you will need:

Eight tablespoons of happiness
Three spoonfuls of joy
Two and a half bottles of essence of cat
Three books
A blonde wig
Two blue marbles
Five baggy jumpers
Seven tablespoons of grumpiness
And lastly
Two spoonfuls of sunshine.

Method:

Microwave the sunshine, the joy and the marbles and then mix in the baggy jumpers and grumpiness.
Add in everything else and bake in the oven.

WARNING: if any worries or nightmares are added, I will become anxious.
MUST: trap worries and nightmares in a jar.

Do you realise how hard it is to create me?
That's right, you can't.
I am unique. This is me.

Aurora Hanlon (9)
Ibstock Place School, Roehampton

Can You Guess Who This Is?

I'm kind and caring,
I'm a rockstar on the drums,
I'm as fast as Dina Asha Smith,
My eyes are the shimmering sea,
I have been stung by a load of bees.

I have three psychotic brothers,
They make me go so crazy,
And even sometimes a little bit lazy,
I don't really like the dresses,
And I certainly don't like cleaning up.

I really love sport,
especially if I play on a diamond blue court,
I really love leopards, tortoises and dogs,
Can you guess what country I'm from?
They love windmills, tulips and clogs,
Yes, you've guessed it, it's Holland.

This is only a bit of me,
Can you guess if I'm a she or a he?

Rafi Brenninkmeijer (9)
Ibstock Place School, Roehampton

This Is Me

Ingredients
A dash of rose-red chocolate
Seven chickens
Seven Horrible History books
A sprinkle of Roblox
Two teaspoons of kindness
One teaspoon of shyness
A ton of glitter

Add the dash of rose-red chocolate with a sprinkle of Roblox and mix
Mix the two teaspoons of kindness with the one teaspoon of shyness
If needed add a dash of fun
Add the seven chickens with the horrible history books and mix with everything else
Pour into a cake tin and put into an oven at thirty-two degrees for one hour
Take it out and leave for twenty minutes
Then add a ton of glitter to make it shine as bright as a diamond
This is me.

Grace McTaggart (8)
Ibstock Place School, Roehampton

This Is Me

I'm a daughter,
With two older brothers,
I bring much laughter,
My face is like my mother's.

When school ends,
My bed takes over,
Slowly my back bends,
Sleep is like a four-leaf clover.

Music soothes me,
The same goes with food,
Music makes me free,
But it always depends on the mood.

I love the summer, it's so much fun,
I'd always get to lay,
Underneath the sun,
and the sky is never grey.

Life is almost never-ending,
Living the best, happily,
Would be a memory, everlasting,
Cherish the moment, positively.

I am a daughter,
And I adore me,
I bring to the table,
Speciality.

Tory Song (10)
Ibstock Place School, Roehampton

This Is Me

I am...

A sister of one big brother
I have a dog, a tiny one
I enjoy equestrian jumping
And I love to run

Swimming is fun, I'm in the squad
Dancing, basketball and other sports I do
I'm on the school team
For netball, gymnastics and volleyball too

I love dogs and know all their breeds
I do daily dog walking
My neighbours have a dog
And we both love talking

Ibstock is the school I go to
Mostly it's fun
Sometimes it's boring
But that is when there is no sun

I'm optimistic, joyful and funny
Helpful, caring and kind
In me and my big smile
Those are the characteristics you'll find.

Emma Kovalchuk (10)
Ibstock Place School, Roehampton

This Is Me

To make this poem you will need:

A dash of excitement,
A tablespoon of fun,
A bowl of helpfulness,
A bag of bright hearts,
A classroom of mischief!

Stir well, then add:

A house of creativity,
A garden full of adventures,
A field of friendliness,
A school full of hard work,
A stadium of superb defence and nifty footwork!

Simmer gently...

The final ingredients are:

A county of pleases and thank yous,
A country of animal adoration,
An ocean full of friends,
A world complete with love.

Now you have made it this far,
All you have to do is chant, "This is me!"

William Rettie (10)
Ibstock Place School, Roehampton

I Am

I am a brother
I am a song
I'm a part of a family
Together we're one

I'm a leader
I am a light
I am a human
That stands up for what's right

I am a musician
I learn how to play
Beautiful songs that will brighten your day

I am a captain
I'm part of a team
I never give up
On achieving my dreams

I am a friend
I'll lend you a hand
You can tell me your worries
And I'll understand

I am a star
Up high in the sky
I know that to shine
I just have to try

I am a person
I am a boy
I will do my best
To bring people joy.

Kit Kroft (10)
Ibstock Place School, Roehampton

All About Me

My name is Imogen and I have blue eyes and brown hair
I'm funny I'm kind
I like watching TV
I have lots of friends
I'm clever and good at art
I love to read and draw
Petting my dog and eating
This is me.
I'm good at French
I have an older sister, she's the best
She's in Year 6
This is me.
I'm small
I play the piano
My family own two beach houses
This is me.
I like travelling and nature
I come from the USA
That's very far away
This is me.

I love playing with my toys
I am confident
I'm not very good at rhyming
I am good at swimming
This is me.

Imogen Kilshaw (8)
Ibstock Place School, Roehampton

I Am Me

I am kind and keen to please,
I love to set people at ease,
I am supportive like a friend,
I love calm and peace.

Everything I say is truthful,
I am a maid to who I meet,
Loyal and polite,
I am a machine to make things neat.

I am strong and brave,
I can do anything if I try,
I can climb any mountain,
I can reach the sky.

I am talented and a believer,
I can soar through the sky,
I am as clever as an owl,
I reach for the stars.

I am loved and cherished,
By all I meet,
Anxious and upset sometimes,
But cheerful and sweet.

I am proud of my imperfect self,
I am me.

Emmeline Anderson (10)
Ibstock Place School, Roehampton

This Is Me

To create me you will need:

Four ounces of sugar (I have lots of energy!)
Two tablespoons of milk
Ten grams of excitement
Mix thoroughly for five minutes
Bake for ten minutes until golden brown
Two ounces of silliness
White icing with a hint of fun
Add a sprinkle of kindness
Rainbow candles.

Now you need to:

Mix the milk with the sugar
Add ten grams of excitement
Mix it for five minutes
Bake it in the oven until it's golden brown
Add the silliness!
Put on the white creamy icing
Add a sprinkle of kindness and fun
Stick the vibrant candles in so they are nice and secure.

Gabriella Lumley (8)
Ibstock Place School, Roehampton

A Recipe For Me

To create me you will need:

Ten tablespoons of dogs
Three pots of paint
One rainbow
One gallon of chocolate
A kind caring family
Five amazing friends

Firstly, get the three pots of paint and add ten tablespoons of dogs into it, whisk it together
Then add the rainbow, leave it on the stove for five minutes
When that's done, add a tiny bit of the scrumptious chocolate, keep going until it's all done
Now, carefully put it in the oven, sprinkle some amazing friends on top,
Don't forget the kind, caring family.
This is me.
Could you do it? That's right, you couldn't!
I'm unique!

Aria Kathuria (9)
Ibstock Place School, Roehampton

Myself

I'm sweet I'm kind
Sometimes I'm shy, I'm different to the class
But I don't mind
I'm as short as my friend
But I'm still not the same
My eyes are deep green
Like the leaves out of the windowpane
My hair is wavy
But when there's a gust of wind
I have lots of favourite subjects
They're really so fun
I like to play fun instruments
But I'm not quite done
I have siblings that are annoying
But I still play with them a lot
I love being me
Even if I'm very cheeky
My favourite sport is gymnastics
Because I'm really stretchy
This is me!

Scarlett Levy (8)
Ibstock Place School, Roehampton

How To Make Me

You will need:

A muddy football
A loud microphone
A Harry Potter book
A video game controller
A swimming cap
And a sprinkle of funny
Firstly, crush some ice
Then add the football
If it is not muddy it will not be chocolatey
Thirdly plop in the loud as a lion microphone
Stir for fifteen seconds
Next, add the Harry Potter book
Then play some video games and then put in the video controller
After that, do some swimming and then add the cap
Lastly, add a sprinkle of funny

Warning: if you add too much funny, the ice cream will be laughing hysterically.

Milly Carter (8)
Ibstock Place School, Roehampton

This Is Me

Ingredients to make me:

A sprinkle of climbing
A handful of reading
A dash of kindness
Twenty-one pounds of food
Ten kilograms of holiday
A bowlful of learning
Seven and a half teaspoons of playing
A bucketful of happiness

Method:

Pour in a dash of kindness.
Add a handful of reading.
Let it simmer with a basketful of happiness.
Add ten kilograms of holiday and a sprinkle of climbing.
Bake the mixture with five teaspoons of playing and twenty-one pounds of food.

Let it cool down and leave with a bowlful of learning.
Bon appetit.

This is me!

Nikolai Jönsson (8)
Ibstock Place School, Roehampton

Me

Super great mind
Supremely kind
Have a great breath
But scared of death
I am sometimes mad
But never sad
I am not hairy
But I am scary
I love the ocean
I have a very fast motion
I have two kittens
And some mittens
I am extremely fun
And have a great pun
I'm bad at the tango
But I eat lots of mangos
I'm as fast as a cheetah
After the race, I can drink a litre
I'm endlessly energetic
Sometimes need a medic

I love coding
It's boring when it says loading
My friend list is long
I'm great at ping-pong
This is me!

Isaac Anand (9)
Ibstock Place School, Roehampton

This Is Me

To create me you will need:

4 ounces of sugar (I have a lot of energy!)
2 tablespoons of milk
10 grams of excitement
3 sprinkles of silliness
White icing with a hint of fun
A pinch of kindness
Decorations

Now you need to:

Mix milk with sugar
Add the 10 grams of excitement
Mix for 5 minutes
Bake in the oven until it's golden brown
Drop the silliness in
Layer it in white creamy icing
Add the kindness
Put the colourful, vibrant decorations on top

Now you should have a cake covered in everything you could imagine about me!

Gabriella Lumley
Ibstock Place School, Roehampton

All About Me

This is me,
Wild and kind,
I have a creative mind,
Swimming is my superpower,
But running makes me cower.

Sweet and sour,
Depending on the hour,
I have a bright smile,
Because I brush my teeth for a while.

I am always very fun,
But my least favourite thing is the fun run,
I'll make a riot,
But then I'll be quiet.

I am a drama queen,
My family and I are the dream team.

So this is me,
Sometimes sad, mostly happy,
And to bring bad moods to a super quick end,
I rely on my amazing gang of lunatic friends.

Holly Flowers (11)
Ibstock Place School, Roehampton

This Is Me

When at play, I buzz around like a bee
However while at work, I try to work hard
But sometimes I am not always good
I like abstract art and superb science
But I dislike too much running, it's an annoyance
When I grow up I want to be a website scripter
However it might be too difficult for me to bother
I have pitch-black hair, I like it neat like me
I dislike complicated clothing, simplicity is key
Foods I like are ruby-red apples
Crimson-red lobster and other things that keep me well fed
So now you know who I am
I am me, you cannot copy me
I am unique.

Lukas Lau (10)
Ibstock Place School, Roehampton

This Is Me

My talent is ballet,
I like singing songs when I'm alone,
My favourite thing about me is that I am flexible,
My dream for the future is to become a ballerina,
When I feel sad I like to be alone,
Bunnies are my favourite animal,
They hop like a kangaroo,
My favourite colour is orange,
I am a magnificent climber,
Art is my favourite lesson,
I play the violin and it makes me happy,
My hair is as brown as soil,
My skin is ancient white,
My favourite toys are Angely and Little White,
I am always on about me, looking nice, my eyes are brown.

Athena Karamanou (10)
Ibstock Place School, Roehampton

How To Make Me

How to make me,
First, add two cups of glee,
One cup of brightness,
With a kilogram of kindness,

Then stir in a teaspoon of fondness for kind-hearted dogs,
Sieve in the brains of a clever clog,
Then add lots of friends that are as sweet as mangoes,
Mix in eyes as brown as banjos,

Include a dog who has stinky breath,
Who creeps on me and scares me to death,
Place in ten books full of glee,
I will read them happily,
Once bubbling, mix in mischief and fun,
And I will get it done,
Bon appetite,
This is how you make me.

Meher Sethi (8)
Ibstock Place School, Roehampton

This Is Me

I love pandas, they're fluffy,
I don't like mushrooms because they're disgusting,
I like sports because it's fun,
I don't like peas because they're not yum,
I love history because it's interesting,
I don't like cabbage because it tastes like a painting,
I like reading books because I like stories,
And I don't like a very loud lorry,
I like computing because we play games,
And I also like doing swimming in lanes,
I'm as happy as a ray of sun without mist,
Do you know who this is?
It's me!

Yinuo Pu (10)
Ibstock Place School, Roehampton

Differences

Who believes that I won't try?
If you ever did, can I ask you why?

Being me means you will always try again,
Even if it looks like it is the end.

I'm vibrant, excited, strong and kind,
But those are only some traits you'll find;

Hidden beneath confidence there is some
Anxiety lurking behind
Although this isn't all I am,
You should really understand,
This is me,
This is who I am,
Even if people don't understand,
Nobody can change me,
This is me,
A person no one else can be.

Fenella Houlihan (11)
Ibstock Place School, Roehampton

This Is Me

To make me you will need:

Eighty grams of love
A dash of Ariana Grande's fashion sense
Three kilograms of stylish bedroom
A never-ending supply of good vibes
Four litres of pure, heartfelt kindness
Thee kilograms of immense bravery

Find an enormous pot and empty in the bedroom and the supply of good vibes
Add in the crumbly love, the kindness and the bravery
Pop in the dash of fashion
That's not all
There are many other things that make up unique me
But everyone is different in some way.

Alessia Fantuzzi (8)
Ibstock Place School, Roehampton

Me And My Life

I am not alien or an animal
I am human
Brown hair, blue eyes
And a bubbling personality

Life isn't a maths question
You can't rub out the mistakes
Be proud of who you are
Stand out and be loud

I'm not anybody's puppet
I am who I am
Nobody can control me
As this is me

Life is like a rollercoaster
It has ups and downs
Don't hide your imperfections
Be passionate and bold

Nobody is perfect
You're perfect in your own way
This is me.

Trephena Glanville (10)
Ibstock Place School, Roehampton

My Me Box

Look inside my box,
It is quite a wonder!
I love to laugh and sing,
I love my family with all my heart,
My friends cheer me up when I am sad.

I fancy a bit of disco,
And I am a bit grumpy too,
I have a soft spot for music,
I have a gigantic sweet tooth!
I am a big believer in magic,
I play the violin, that is true!

I have diamond blue eyes,
Blonde hair like the sun,
It does not like to be brushed!
Some rainbows inside,
And a bunny too,
Here is your surprise,
It is me!

Isla Roberts (9)
Ibstock Place School, Roehampton

This Is Me

My resilience is as hard as coal,
It helps me to rock and roll!
I am friendly and love my food,
If I eat it, it will instantly brighten my mood.
Music is my talent and with my four instruments I have fun,
I also enjoy the thrill of dancing in the sun!
I am also an excellent scuba diver,
However, I am not old enough to be a driver.
I love sketching and art lessons,
Drawing is so fun and my stress lessens.
I do so many clubs after school,
I find doing them really cool!
This is me,
Someone only I can be.

Eric Zeng (10)
Ibstock Place School, Roehampton

All About Me

This is all about me,
About what I like
What emotions I have,
How often I ride my bike.

First of all,
I ride my bike every day,
Even when outside it's grey.

I like cheese puffs, they're delicious.
I love snow,
And here are my wishes:
I wish for a happy home,
For a peaceful world.
I wish for crepes,
And for my hair to be a bit curled.

My feelings change,
I guess I'm not always happy,
Sometimes I'm sad,
But after all,
This poem is about me.

Maria Steier (10)
Ibstock Place School, Roehampton

This Is Me

T he thing that makes me happy is reading books in my bed
H aving a pet is always my dream but it's in my head
I love playing tennis with my dad, but sometimes he gets moody
S pace is one of the things that interests me

I want to be a scientist when I grow up
S ometimes when my teacher talks about the body parts I say shut up

M ischievous, not dumb and very fun
E xciting fun and I am never done.

Quiet as a mouse and soon you will see
This is me!

Alessandro
Ibstock Place School, Roehampton

This Is Me

I'm quiet, gentle and polite,
But don't make me angry, watch out I bite,
I'm wild, daring and full of life,
I try to avoid all conflict and strife,

You'll see me in a corner, immersed in a book,
I may seem timid but that's just a look,
Underneath I am,
A writer, writing, a painter painting, a hiker hiking,
And a creator creating,
I'm apprehensive and afraid,
These are traits I'd rather trade,
But these are all parts of me,
This is who I am meant to be,
This is me.

Ella Schoelzel Sipahi (10)
Ibstock Place School, Roehampton

This Is Me

I'm a secretive clam,
And I dislike glam,
I'm happy, I'm sad,
But if you're my friend you'll be glad.
I love to strike along the glistening pitch,
And it's my hobby to play on my switch.

I always try hard a lot,
But when I don't it looks like simple dots.
I'm as bright as a shining rainbow,
And when I get to school I feel a glow,
I have a few insecurities, it's not the best feeling,
But it's who I'm meant to be,
I really love my life.
This is me.

Maya Peters (9)
Ibstock Place School, Roehampton

My Life

I like school but some lessons make me drool.
Sometimes they're fun and I never want them to be done.
My favourite lesson is sport and I love running around the court.
My favourite sport is football and every day I kick a ball against a wall.

I am as fast as a cheetah, I am as kind as a rose.
I am kind, funny and never boast.
My eyes are brown, my face is tanned.
I really like my feet in the sand.

I love my life, it is really amazing.
And what makes it more fun is that my friends are entertaining!

Jake Ballantyne (9)
Ibstock Place School, Roehampton

This Is Me

This is me,
A proud son,
A nice brother,
Always having fun.

My hair is brown like caramel,
My teeth are very crooked,
My eyes as green as emerald.

Like a star shining brightly,
I stand out in the crowd,
A fighting knight,
I never give up.

My sister would say,
I'm always annoying,
But I smile every day,
Trying to bring everyone joy.

This is me,
It would be a dull world if we were all the same,
But we are all unique,
And we will always be.

Gaspar Velasco (11)
Ibstock Place School, Roehampton

Football

Football is my game,
I play it every day,
It wakes my neighbours up,
And my favourite video game is FIFA 22,
I love to play all sports,
Except for netball and tennis,
Those are the games I dislike the most,
Neymar Jr is my favourite player,
I am as fast as a F1 car,
And as tough as a cricket ball,
And as rough as a brick wall,
No one can get past me,
I am as cool as a tough guy,
I have brown shiny hair,
I get up very early,
It annoys my parents a lot,
I am good at sports.

Noah Beattie (8)
Ibstock Place School, Roehampton

If I Were Perfect

If I were perfect
It wouldn't be me
In fact, it wouldn't be anyone
It just couldn't be

If I were perfect
I would do my homework on time
Tying my own laces
Or even learn how to rhyme

If I were perfect
I would make myself a tool
Share some open views
Could possibly ride a bike to school

But being imperfect isn't so bad
And there is no reason to be sad
Because to my parents, I am perfect
Perfect in my own unique imperfect way.

Kiran Mahan (10)
Ibstock Place School, Roehampton

Amazing Anoushka

I am a fox, I'm quick and strong,
If you ever doubted me, I'd say you were wrong.
I am one of a kind, I am unique,
I love every single day of the week!
I am weird,
But I certainly don't have a beard.
My favourite place to be is definitely down by the sea,
My very best friend of course that's Georgie!
When I get home from school I play outside,
I must say my dog is very wide.
I've dreaded this moment, I'm sorry my friends,
But this is where our story ends.

Anoushka Green (9)
Ibstock Place School, Roehampton

This Is Me

Ingredients
A million grams of cheekiness
A handful of love for football
A pinch of flammable powder
The bright sun

A smidge of annoyance
A large school of laughter
A pot of pessimistic thinking
The twinkling stars

A whole classroom filled with enthusiasm
A bowl of dark humour
A thousand joke books
The word fun

I'm not going to tell you the method because I don't want you to make me
In fact you will never make me,
I am unique!

Francisco Daganski-Evans (9)
Ibstock Place School, Roehampton

This Is Me

Everyone has a name
Everyone has a culture
Everyone has a dream and inspiration
So do I

My name is Thomas Petrou, I have a brother
My family are from Greece
Funny, cheeky, energetic, these words describe me

Football, music, gaming and making people laugh are my likes
In football, I can lose my temper

I am a wizard on the pitch, I am a chatty comedian
Not gonna lie, eat a lot of sweets
This is my life
This is what makes me who I am
This is me.

Thomas Petrou (10)
Ibstock Place School, Roehampton

Learning About Me

My favourite ice cream topping is Oreo,
And my favourite holiday is Christmas, ho ho ho!
This is me!
My hair is curly when it's dry and straight when it's wet,
Did I mention I'm in the top maths set,
This is me!
I have two brothers,
And no others,
This is me!
My dog is called Rey,
And I love to swim by the bay,
This is me!
Sometimes I am as silent as a snake,
And other times I am a boisterous as a baboon,
So for the last time…
This is me!

Ella Smith (9)
Ibstock Place School, Roehampton

This Is Me

Hanna is my name,
I am the opposite of lame,
Me and my kitty are best friends,
I like to cycle by the River Thames,
My hair is short and chestnut-brown,
I live in a city, not a town,
I am usually very crazy,
But sometimes just a little lazy,
Sometimes I disobey my mum and say no,
Christmas is my favourite, ho ho ho,
I like to chew little things,
I love it when my doorbell rings,
I find it helpful when my friends give me critique,
This is me,
I am unique.

Hanna Ghods (8)
Ibstock Place School, Roehampton

This Is Me

My name is Paloma
I'm an excellent cook
In the kitchen you'll find me
My head in a book

I go to Ibstock Place School
It's a very nice place
It makes me laugh
And puts a smile on my face

I've made lots of good friends
That I'll never forget
"Friends for life," we say, you bet!

For my life, I'm ambitious
I don't follow the crowd
My aim is to improve the world
And make my parents proud.

Paloma Gwyer (10)
Ibstock Place School, Roehampton

This Is Me

This is me, Sophia is my name
And I love when my grandparents come
In my spare time I like to see the bright sky as the birds go by

This is me, I like to sew and I like to watch my favourite show
I am good at jumping across my grandparents' house
But while doing that I scream when I see a tiny mouse

This is me, I think that going to school is lucky
I always feel jolly

This is me, I love to play with my friends
I love to learn new things.

Sophia Cho (8)
Ibstock Place School, Roehampton

I Am

I am a cousin, a sister and a daughter,
Making every soul smile.
To achieve this amazing goal,
I don't need to run a mile.

I am a leader,
I am a funny jolly friend.
If you need some help,
I've got a hand to lend.

I am a star,
Shining brightly in the sky.
I will be there for every sigh,
And comfort every cry.

I may not be perfect,
But I love me.
So why don't you sit down,
And then you will see.

Maria Isabel Buyo (10)
Ibstock Place School, Roehampton

This Is Me

I open my eyes while the alarm bell is ringing,
I stumble downstairs to breakfast.
I collect everything I need to bring,
And we can leave at last.

I jump into the car ready for a long drive,
As fast as a racing car along the motorway.
I know I will have to strive,
I just hope I go the right way.

When we get there I hop on my bike,
I set up as quick as possible.
I am so nervous about the pike,
Then the fear starts to nibble.

William Lambert (10)
Ibstock Place School, Roehampton

This Is Me

Isobel is my name
Monopoly is my favourite board game
I'm as fast as a horse
And as cuddly as a bear
I've also got brown hair
I'm as gentle as a butterfly
Like a monkey I am cheeky
I also do lots of things cheerfully
My favourite animal is a red panda
Even though my name is Isobel I like the name Amanda
I am someone you can trust
But sometimes I must
Disobey my mum and say no
When people say I've lied, I say so?

Isobel Dajani (9)
Ibstock Place School, Roehampton

Me

I have a name
But I'm unique
I don't bask in fame

You can have a peek
At me, a real child
But I am unique

My temper seems extremely mild
But beware it might not be
I am just a mere child

Already swimming in the world surrounding me
It is cool
My world, I guess, is very happy

I am not a fool
No
I go to school
Oh

I exist, I stand out, I read books
I am unique!

Denis Rodionov (9)
Ibstock Place School, Roehampton

This Is Me

This is me, I am strong
I am happy, dragging my cello along
I am smart, I am kind
Dig deep and you will find
The supportive, mature, crazy and weird
The girl who is never feared
Energetic, sporty and funny
Social and silly, just like a bee who loves its honey
I am loveable, excited and funky
Just like a silly monkey
I am mature, I am loud
I am creative, I am proud
I am fearless, I am smiley
I am awesome
This is me.

Poppy Letting (10)
Ibstock Place School, Roehampton

Ingredients To Make Me

To make me you will need:

A touch of cupcakes
A sprinkle of glitter
Lime and lemon
As well as a slice of hot cheesy pizza
A pound of sugar and a pinch of spice
Don't forget kindness or it won't be nice

Some sage and thyme as well as fries to share
And don't forget the sauce
Never add rudeness or you will have a real scare
As quick as you can add more pizza
Add a pinch of laughter like a funny hyena.

Eudora Wawra (8)
Ibstock Place School, Roehampton

This Is Me

I am friendly but quiet,
Creative and kind,
I am passionate and respectful,
As well as thoughtful and shy.
I am adaptable and polite,
Determined, accepting and approachable,
I am mature and understanding,
Also resourceful and positive,
But I am also stressed,
And anxious and scared,
I am a swimmer, a dancer, an artist and a cook,
Everyone is different, unique.
You are the only you,
And I am the only me.

Sibylla Coleman (11)
Ibstock Place School, Roehampton

This Is Me

My name is Noah and I like football,
I'm pretty good and I'm super tall,
I am a cheeky cheetah,
A great gorilla too,
I think I'm super cool,
But I don't have a swimming pool,
I love pizza, it's my favourite food,
But I really dislike people who are rude,
So that's pretty much me,
Always with my family,
I don't like spinach because it's kinda gross,
Though I do like jam on toast.

Noah Streule (9)
Ibstock Place School, Roehampton

This Is Me

K atya is my name, so this is me
A rt, tennis, crochet, football, I like them a lot
T oday I am one, tomorrow I'm another
Y ou say I am small as an ant
A nd I have luscious golden hair

I have eyes that are like oceans
S ometimes I can cause a commotion

M y friendship is strong and forever will be
E veryone is different and this poem is about me.

Katerina Godunova (9)
Ibstock Place School, Roehampton

I Am A Superstar

My name is Hollie
I love eating lollies
I am great and nobody can hate me
Because I am ten out of ten
I want to go to Big Ben
I am not very tall but I am bright
And I don't ever want to fight
I'm not perfect I am kind
And I don't mind veggies, they are pretty cool
No, I am not a fool,
I don't care about winning
I don't care about losing
I am jumpy like a flea
This is me!

Hollie Hughes (9)
Ibstock Place School, Roehampton

This Is Me

I am as jolly as a joker,
As cheeky as a chimp,
I'm a super speed creator,
And a brilliant baker,
I'm a deadly defender,
And an incredible inventor,
I am as silent as a mouse,
And my hand is keen for doodles,
I love to play computer games,
And my favourite food is cake,
My brother is named Ben,
And he is as silly as a hen,
I love my dog called Poppy,
But Covid tests suck.

Sam Hilsley (10)
Ibstock Place School, Roehampton

Me

My hair is chocolate-brown, I wonder if you knew
My eyes are light blue
I like my freckles too
I like my purple glue

PE is my time
I like to get to the finish line
Running races is such a pleasure
I do swimming for leisure

Netball is my favourite game
You need to see me aim
Hockey is my second favourite sport
I like hitting the ball in the court.

This is me.

Freya Bittan (9)
Ibstock Place School, Roehampton

How To Make Me

To make me you will need:

A tumble load of TV,
A pinch of aromatic ginger,
A truckload of swimming,
A swipe of tasty noodles,
A handful of grammar mistakes,
A dozen interesting books,
A sprinkle of laughter,
A tornado of courage,
Half a teaspoon of abstract art,
A gallon of fizzing energy,
A bottle of shyness,
An explosion of fun,
Two murky marbles,
This is me.

Evangeline Sochovsky (10)
Ibstock Place School, Roehampton

Me

T old I am smart
H appy but hard
I love football, pets and my friends too
S ometimes I'm grumpy but not around you

I 've got curly maple hair, turquoise eyes
S inging and dancing never lies

M e and my friends have so much fun
E xciting wonder until the day is done!

Mischievous like a monkey,
But soon you'll see!

Izzy Houlihan (9)
Ibstock Place School, Roehampton

This Is Me

I am as little as a dwarf,
As fun as a game,
I have hair as dark as the twilight dime,
I am a lover of animals,
My family is my joy,
I specialise in ramen,
I'm as noisy as a frog,
I'm as silly as a pog,
As clever as a fox,
As quick as a cheetah,
I love my friends,
My favourite colour is red,
And the cat is my animal,
I have no pets though,
This is me.

Rosetta Weng (9)
Ibstock Place School, Roehampton

This Is Me

I love to draw
As my pencil dances on the page
I am a shooting star
In the goal defence netball bib
I love sports as I dance and leap on the court

I can swim like a plane
Shooting through the sapphire sky
I love history and learning about the past
My favourite is the gory Greeks
My hair is a gradient from blonde to brown
My eyes are the deep ferocious sea
This is me.

Robyn Taskis (10)
Ibstock Place School, Roehampton

About Me

My name is Andreas,
And I'm here to say,
I'm the best football player in the team today,
Your defenders are fast,
But my dribbling is faster,
Haha,
I scored,
They call me the master,
My hair is blonde and brown,
And I live in the town,
And I never let my football team down,
I've got a brother,
Who's younger than me,
And screams as loud as a siren!

Andreas Anagnostopulos (9)
Ibstock Place School, Roehampton

This Is Owen

Grateful, kind,
Really fast mind,
Maths is my superpower,
Lunch is my favourite hour,
I play football because it's fun,
I never stop until I'm done,
I am positive as much as I can,
In the summer I have a dark tan,
In the winter I am always tired,
I love Christmas, it's really been admired,
Ah yes I love it when it snows,
Presents are the best, everybody knows.

Owen Herpers (10)
Ibstock Place School, Roehampton

About Me

This is me, I am good at football but not at all sport
I adore strawberry cake but not to bake
My name is Federico but you may call me Rico
When I'm sad there is always my lovely dad
They say I'm funny but bouncy like a bunny
My brother says I'm annoying but I don't think I am
Fed is also my name and I love Monopoly as a board game
I don't like hot cross buns, nor to run.

Federico Cortinovis (9)
Ibstock Place School, Roehampton

A Little Bit Of Me

A little bit of funny
The legs of a bunny
A little bit of smart
A little bit of art
A little bit of rugby
You can't not love me
A little bit of rock
I don't like to mock
At first, I can be frightful
Once you know me I'm delightful
A little bit of skiing
From an avalanche, I'm fleeing
A little bit of reading
Because literacy is very important!

Rafe Bolger (8)
Ibstock Place School, Roehampton

I Am Me

My hair is golden like the sun
You will find a smile on my face
My favourite food is a schnitzel
Second on my list is a pretzel

I love my fluffy dog
Who jumps around in bogs
Food and sleep are my main ambition
It is a British tradition

Cycling and sailing are my hobbies
I barely have any worries
I love travelling from place to place
With a big suitcase.

Oscar Homerstone (10)
Ibstock Place School, Roehampton

This Is Me

T errifically kind like a BFG,
H appy with most things that happen to me,
I magination is big and strong,
S ticky toffee pudding is my favourite pudding and has been for so long,

I nterested in the war with planes that crash down,
S illy as a jovial clown,

M usical like Freddie Mercury,
E xcellent skateboarder like Tony Hawk.

Dylan Phillips (10)
Ibstock Place School, Roehampton

This Is Me

I'm as sneaky as a snake
I'm a marvellous baker making a mouth-watering cake

I'm a clumsy boy, dropping objects as I go
I'm a messy person, stacking toys to and fro

I'm a history lover, filling myself with facts
I'm sporty and energetic, hitting balls with bats

I'm a reader, warped in a book
I'm a light sleeper and here I am, look!

Ryan Choi (10)
Ibstock Place School, Roehampton

This Is Me

I am a strong asset,
With a positive mindset.

Sports is my inspiration to do well,
It always motivates me to feel swell.

I am enthusiastic about football,
I hope my determination will lead me above all.

I enjoyed participating in a charity run,
The 600-metre sprint was exhaustingly fun.

Energetic, thoughtful and kind,
I never feel left behind.

Ali Charchafchi (11)
Ibstock Place School, Roehampton

My Peculiar Poem

I have brown hair
I love pears
I am Irish, Kiwi and Dutch
I always want to touch

Can't write a great poem
So hard to rhyme, have to make up words like 'soem'
I love my friends
Even though they drive me around the bend

Great with guitar
I always want to go to Qatar
Perfect with the piano
I love to think of words like 'tiano'.

Henry O'Donnell (10)
Ibstock Place School, Roehampton

Me

I come from a land far away,
That we call the USA,

My eyes are blue, my hair is blonde,
My friends and I have tight bonds,

I'm funny, loving and always true,
Hates and dislikes, I have a few,

On the outside, I may seem small,
But on the inside, I always stand tall,

I am kind, thoughtful and very sweet,
To be around me is quite a treat.

Maren-Amelie Kilshaw (10)
Ibstock Place School, Roehampton

This Is Me

T his is me, when I'm happy I'm also kind
H ello, I say when I see someone
I get hot when I wear my cosy sweater
S ometimes I am happy

I n France, I get freezing cold, but in Greece, I get very hot
S o when I do origami I always fold

M y favourite animal is a dog
E verywhere in a park, I search for a log.

Arion-Derin Paparizos (8)
Ibstock Place School, Roehampton

How To Make Me

To make me you will need:

10 sprinkles of strength
45 ounces of speed
25 grams of silliness
One steaming hot slab of pizza.

Method:

Mix the hot slab of pizza with 45 ounces of speed
Then add the 25 grams of silliness and bake for 15 minutes
Then add the 10 sprinkles of strength

Voila! But what have you made?

Me!

Hasan Al-Khatib
Ibstock Place School, Roehampton

Me

Leonardo is my name
Football is my favourite game
I'm always very happy and helpful
But sometimes I'm as cheeky as a monkey
I'm as fast as a Ferrari
And also really kind
Oh did I tell you, I'm also colour blind?
And finally, I have a very smart mind
I could also find
A treasure chest in the depths of the sea

That's me!

Leonardo Di Dio (8)
Ibstock Place School, Roehampton

I'm Like This

This is me
I'm as small as a munching mouse
I'm as happy as a perfect purring panther
This is me
I'm scared like a rabbit
I'm as clever as an octopus
This is me
I'm as chatty as a partying parakeet
I'm as hilarious as a hyena
This is me
I'm not as brave as a bear
I'm as fantastic as Mr Fox
This is me.

Jenson Boyd (9)
Ibstock Place School, Roehampton

This Is Me

To make me you will need:

Two cute cats and dogs,
Six big Popits but not too big,
Three chocolate bars but not dark,
One iPad or phone for me to game,
Four fairy wands,
Two big books about maths and English,
A few toys of Hello Kitty,
One pencil case,
Lots of lego and noodles,
Ten pots of paint,
Last of all, friends!

Jing Tong Lyu (9)
Ibstock Place School, Roehampton

This Is Me

My favourite colour is yellow
My eyes are water-blue
My favourite game is netball
You need a lot of aim
My hair is dirty blonde
Like the colour of light wood
I'm quite bubbly, chatty too
But sometimes I can be as quiet as a swift silent spider
My favourite season is winter
It's usually as cold as ice
This is me.

Aurelia O'Connor Lally (8)
Ibstock Place School, Roehampton

This Is Me

Hello this is me
I play football as a goalie
I dive to the left, I dive to the right
Every day I take flight

I am a crazy dreamer, I hit the crash
And it goes bash
I play at school and I have a dog
He's called Leo, he likes to sleep

As I play at night, he runs as crazy as a knight
So that is me!

Andrey Varilow
Ibstock Place School, Roehampton

This Is Me

T ip-top shape, tiniest in the family
H ave too much homework
I always do things happily
S ometimes I play with my mum

I don't like mango, kiwi and plum
S o here I am standing tall and still

M y favourite colour is green
E xciting planter of black beans.

Pedro Henrique Stuckert Weber Dos Santos (8)
Ibstock Place School, Roehampton

This Is Me

I am perfect in my own way,
To my friends, I will always be there and stay.
I am a daughter, student and niece,
I love cooking cakes and I will give you a piece.
I love to play video games,
Gaming and colouring are some of my hobbies.
I sometimes have lots of big worries,
I always end up in a huge hurry.

Lina Tikriti (10)
Ibstock Place School, Roehampton

Me, Myself And I

I am...
Art loving,
Hardworking,
Chit chatter,
Silly swirler,
Social buzzing,
Busy as a bee,
Singer,
Don't linger,
I am a book borrower,
Public speaking makes me cower,
Holiday lover,
Maybe Christmas in summer,
I am a sister and a daughter,
In no particular order.

Hanna Kivinen (10)
Ibstock Place School, Roehampton

This Is Me

I am creative
I like to paint with watercolours
I like to be silly and help others
I am happy with the way I live in my small cramped space
I can do lots and make sure to embrace
All my joy filled up in a full journal
My love for dogs and all animals is eternal
This is me
The only person I can be.

Michaela Tsapralis (10)
Ibstock Place School, Roehampton

My Dog

Her breath smells like candy
She's as loud as a horn
She acts like she's eighty but she was only just born
It's like there's fleet of her
And bites my neighbour Pete Aflore
She eats my socks
And hates rocks
She eats strange things
And jumps like she has wings
I love my dog.

Mason Elwin-Davis (10)
Ibstock Place School, Roehampton

This Is Me

I am a daughter,
I am a sister,

I'm a shining star in the sky,
That shines bright and high,
I am grateful for everything and everyone,
My life is amazing because it's so fun,

I go to the one and only Ibstock Place School,
My favourite place there is definitely the pool.

Sonya Kunts (10)
Ibstock Place School, Roehampton

This Is Me

William is my name
I'm the opposite of lame
Chelsea is my team
I'm also quite lean
I'm as rapid as a race car
And as tall as a giraffe
When I get dirty, I always have a bath
My favourite book is Harry Potter
When the sun is out it just gets hotter and hotter
This is me.

William Cook (9)
Ibstock Place School, Roehampton

Who Am I?

T he awesome, supportive, animal lover,
H appiness is given with kindness.
I n a talented endless cycle,
S illy as a clown.

I am an early riser,
S porty and strong.

M inded with good ideas,
E verything on this list makes me, me.

Leo Hellier (10)
Ibstock Place School, Roehampton

My Life

My name is Huxley and I'm nine years old
My sister is Bella as I was once told

I will soon grow as tall as a tree
I'll always have fun and I'll always be me

I like to play football with all of my friends
We run around crazy until our time ends

This is me!

Huxley Coombes (9)
Ibstock Place School, Roehampton

This Is Me

I am a Lego owner
I own many bricks
I am a milk drinker
My bones are very strong
I am a friend maker
I am never lonely
I am a book reader
I am rarely bored
I am a codebreaker
But there are codes I can't crack
And last but not least
I am a homework hater.

Arthur Tilev-Maroney (8)
Ibstock Place School, Roehampton

All You Will Need

All you will need to make me is:

A ton of speed,
A lot of fun games,
A bucketful of friends,
An annoying brother,
Kind parents,
And of course some art!
And don't forget
A heart and lungs and veins,
I will need some arteries
And blood you know.

Rupert le Roux (9)
Ibstock Place School, Roehampton

This Is Me

T all not small,
H appy with things that happen,
I magination is strong,
S uperbly quick,

I deas are as great as Albert Einstein,
S anitary at all times,

M erry at Christmas time,
E ager to learn in school.

Christopher-John Martin (10)
Ibstock Place School, Roehampton

I Am Myself
A kennings poem

I am a...
Football booter
Shot stopper
Nature viewer
Car admirer
Art creator
Lego builder
Fruit admirer
Blue painter
Infinite explorer
Goal scorer
Nice carer
Red user
Manchester United support
And best of all
Video game player.

Elmar Streule (7)
Ibstock Place School, Roehampton

This Is Me

I am a
Candy eater
Chatty speaker
Food lover
Blanket hogger
Guitar player
Cake maker
Pro swimmer
Rock climber
Puppy owner

I'm an artist in the making
Brilliant at baking
Very late-waking
Soon this poem will be record-breaking.

Isabella Coombes (11)
Ibstock Place School, Roehampton

How To Make Me

To make me you will need:

A pinch of creativity,
A swipe of happiness,
A tablespoon of netball,
A drop of spelling mistakes,
A bowl of pasta,
A quarter of a book, no more,
A dash of Italian,
A swig of Spanish,
A cup of Irish.

Gabriella Blundell (9)
Ibstock Place School, Roehampton

I Am

A kennings poem

A food gobbler
Super swimmer
Kitten owner
Star striker
Mum annoyer
Rapid runner
Animal lover
Assessment acer
Happiness spreader
Basketball beater
Chocolate vanisher
Marvellous musician
Amazing creator.

Kaan Ulgen (10)
Ibstock Place School, Roehampton

Me

A kennings poem

I am a...
Yellow admirer
Cupcake eater
Slope seeker
Water stroker
Cat hater
Garden relaxer
Friend carer
Toe pointer
Music lover
Animal researcher
Colour creator
And lastly
A family protector.

Erin Donovan (7)
Ibstock Place School, Roehampton

This Is Me
A kennings poem

Green killer
Ball player
Goal saver
Star skiller
Superstar shooter
Star dribbler
Footwork spacer
Physical shielder
Speed runner
Super winner
Goal saver
Goal maker
Ball kicker
Leg mover.

Benjamin Whitby-Smith (7)
Ibstock Place School, Roehampton

This Is Me
A kennings poem

This is me...
I am an...
Art admirer
Animal carer
This is me!
I am a...
Toe painter
Flower picker
This is me!
I am a...
Bird watcher
Water stroker
And best of all...
A hard worker.

Cynthia (Xinyue) Zhang (7)
Ibstock Place School, Roehampton

This Is Me
A kennings poem

I am a…
Book reader
Mini gamer
Animal carer
Pop hopper
Jewellery lover
Garment designer
Colourful sketcher
Jumpy skater
Jolly sewer
Jewellery collector
And finally
A great helper!

Xanthe Michael (7)
Ibstock Place School, Roehampton

This Is Me
A kennings poem

I am a...
Slope searcher
Rugby watcher
TV hogger
Fossil admirer
Snow player
Garden relaxer
Ball runner
Animal watcher
Snow sinker
Racket swinger
And finally
A cello player!

Lucas Quin (8)
Ibstock Place School, Roehampton

This Is Me

I am a predator on the field,
I am a running machine,
I am a damage dealer,
I am a mimicking monkey,
I am as jumpy as a jaguar,
I am a shooting star,
I am myself.
Who am I?

This is me.

Max Harrison (9)
Ibstock Place School, Roehampton

Me

A kennings poem

I am a...
Sparkle collector
Art creator
High leaper
Cello player
Pet helper
Amaze maker
Book reader
Cooking maker
Amazing climber
And finally I am a...
Nature explorer.

Delfina Vocos Aguirre (7)
Ibstock Place School, Roehampton

This Is Me
A kennings poem

I am a...
Racket slicer
Animal explorer
Horse trotter
Wood carver
Dog hugger
Cricket smasher
Art splasher
Bike stunter
Piano player
And finally...
A foot sprinter.

Grayston Conroy (7)
Ibstock Place School, Roehampton

Me

A kennings poem

I am...
An animal carer
A master builder
A card collector
A slope seeker
A ball kicker
A water stroker
A melody maker
A leg mover
And finally
An English learner!

Alessandro Jacob Shamim (7)
Ibstock Place School, Roehampton

This Is Me

A kennings poem

I am an...

Early riser,
Dog lover,
Chocolate eater,
Light sleeper,
Deep thinker,
Football supporter,
Video game player,
Overall...
A good friend!

Hugh Smith (11)
Ibstock Place School, Roehampton

Being Myself
A kennings poem

I am a...
Snow player
Family walker
Slope slipper
Wildlife watcher
Colour bug collector
Plant carer
Quick mover
And finally
A football watcher.

Celina Poshkus (7)
Ibstock Place School, Roehampton

This Is Me
A kennings poem

I am a...
Back bender
Colourful picker
Slope searcher
Cross rail jumper
Animal freer
Word reader
Seashell collector
And finally
A hard worker.

Carine Levy (7)
Ibstock Place School, Roehampton

Me

A kennings poem

I am a...
Race winner
Height basher
TV hogger
Animal carer
School councillor
Man City follower
Fossil admirer
And finally
A fearless leader.

Felix George O'Donnell (7)
Ibstock Place School, Roehampton

What I Love
A kennings poem

I am a…
Nature admirer
Book reader
Food eater
Art creator
Tree climber
Snow skier
And finally
A joy maker.

Isabella Zavos (7)
Ibstock Place School, Roehampton

Me

A kennings poem

Video player
Super kicker
Quick finger
Master kicker
Strong lifter
Smart thinker
Funny feature
Cute player.

Benjamin Vocus (7)
Ibstock Place School, Roehampton

About Me

A kennings poem

I am a...
Story lover
Kind thinker
Cat stroker
Drawing lover
Speed craver
Fast thinker
Super kicker.

Felix Currie (7)
Ibstock Place School, Roehampton

Me

A kennings poem

Super kicker
Good stroker
Breath holder
Lycra wearer
Water lover
Goggle wearer
This is me.

Ellie Howarth-Saunders (7)
Ibstock Place School, Roehampton

This Is Me
A kennings poem

I am a...
Pedal spinner
Car dodger
Helmet wearer
Speedy glider
Swift mover
Slip streamer.

Isla Pollock (7)
Ibstock Place School, Roehampton

Football Player
A kennings poem

Goal saver
Goal maker
Ball kicker
Goal scorer
Goal shooter
Goal defender
Goal midfielder.

Naba Hasmi (7)
Ibstock Place School, Roehampton

My Vets
A kennings poem

Animal lover
Food giver
Kindness giver
Fluff stroker
Cuddle giver
Pet lover
This is me!

Sophia Dell (7)
Ibstock Place School, Roehampton

Singing
A kennings poem

Super smiler
Audience facer
Clothes wearer
Song maker
Note traveller
Person pleaser.

Harper Tricker (7)
Ibstock Place School, Roehampton

Me

A kennings poem

Ball hitter
Club chooser
Course player
Ball positioner
Club gripper
Hole winner.

Alice Leonard (7)
Ibstock Place School, Roehampton

This Is Me
A kennings poem

Jolly jumper
Risk taker
Playful pouncer
Ball kicker
Number master
Plan producer.

Luka Taborin (8)
Ibstock Place School, Roehampton

Me
A kennings poem

Rapid runner
Car dodger
Wave rider
Music player
Brave leader
History winner.

Hari Haddock (7)
Ibstock Place School, Roehampton

Beatboxer

A kennings poem

Voice user,
Sound maker,
Mouth mover,
Rhythm changer,
Tongue twister.

Hugo le Roux (7)
Ibstock Place School, Roehampton

This Is Me

When I was little,
I loved to draw,
I loved to sing,
I loved it all.

But something was missing,
What was it?
I didn't know,
But now I'm older,
I understand,
It was something else to do,
With my hand.

It's writing of course!
One of my favourite things to do,
I like it more than television,
I like it more than food! (Kind of.)
I wrote story after story,
And I knew,
I would never get bored,
Of my special thing to do.

But now it's time to put the pen down,
And tell you my story,
My story with challenges,
My story with fun.

Writing stories is still my passion,
But I wanted something new,
Gardening is fun and I like it,
But it's just not something I would do.

That's when I tried basketball,
I was reluctant at first,
But now I keep on playing,
I find it super-duper fun,
In fact I find it so much fun,
I feel like I could burst!

I love reading,
I find it relaxing,
It's very fun to do!
A lot of people like it,
So you should try it too!
I read book after book,
And I never get bored,

It's a super nice thing,
I could get every book in every store!

All of these are still my thing,
But it's only because I tried,
All you have to do is spread your wings,
And you can soar so high.

This is my journey,
It's been challenging and fun,
It seems like a lot,
But it's only just begun.

Saffron Banga (11)
Pool Hayes Primary School, Willenhall

Loud

I'm loud, I'm loud, I'm loud, loud, loud
I like being loud, it's very fun
I'm not loud all the time but most of the time
I'm loud, loud, loud

I'm loud all day long, I never stop
When I'm not being loud it's not very fun
Because I love being loud, loud, loud

And when I read
I'm not just loud, loud, loud
I'm fast, fast, fast
You might think if someone is being loud all day long
That their throat will hurt
Well mine doesn't because
I'm amazing at being loud, loud, loud
And last of all
I'm funny, funny, funny
Nice, nice, nice
And as you know
I'm loud, loud, loud.

Gia Halpin
Pool Hayes Primary School, Willenhall

Reach For The Stars

I'm a girl,
Called Ruby,
Very tall,
And a bit loopy,
I love sports,
I find it entertaining,
Maths,
Very puzzling,
Art,
Creative,
Gymnastics,
Very fun,
But can hurt you a lot,
My mum is Cory,
She reminds me of Finding Dory,
Ryan is my dad,
Sometimes I get him mad,
Amellia is my sister,
Sometimes she gives me a blister,
Oscar is my brother,
Sometimes he acts like my mother,

Next is my nan,
She acts like my biggest fan,
Wendy is my aunty,
Her children are pretty naughty,
That's all about me,
And
My family tree.

Ruby Hewitt (11)
Pool Hayes Primary School, Willenhall

I Love Me

I am Maddie
I love me
I like my phone
I like my friends
But most importantly
I love me
I love my long hair
I love my blue eyes
I love me
And my dad and my mum
Even my sisters
I love my pets
Even when they're smelly
I love me
I love to write
I love to sing
I love to do everything
I love me
Even at the worst times
I love me.

Maddison-Leigh Brittle (10)
Pool Hayes Primary School, Willenhall

Games

Games games games
I love games
Play games every day after school
I play Fortnite, FIFA and football
And lots more
Games are so fun so I play games
For Christmas all I hope I get is
Games, games, games.

Ghianna Jean Parry
Pool Hayes Primary School, Willenhall

Recipe About Me

Ingredients:
A pinch of happiness
A tablespoon of iPad
A lot of sport
A lot of PS4
A hint of playing with my brother
A lot of liking supercars
A scoop of kindness
A hint of silliness

Mix:
Add a pinch of happiness and a scoop of kindness
Then add a tablespoon of iPad and a lot of PS4
After that, add a pinch of playing with my little brother
Add a lot of sport with a hint of silliness
Finally, add a lot of liking supercars to the messy mix
This is me.

Zakariya Ali (11)
Wakefield Methodist Junior & Infant School, Thornes

This Is Me

Sometimes I like green
Then I like blue
I dislike tomatoes but like avocados
I love karate but don't like running
My favourite YouTuber is Quickity, who I watch every night
I have eight siblings and I'm the youngest
My best friend is Jessica who is the best
When I'm energetic there's no point in trying
I'll still be hyper
I'm not a good listener, but I'm a good writer.

Lilac Sherwood (10)
Wakefield Methodist Junior & Infant School, Thornes

All About Me

I'm like a turtle, shy and quiet
But when you get to know me
I can cause a riot
I love my three guinea pigs
Hearing them squeak
Whilst lying on my bed, almost falling asleep
When I get older, being a realtor is my dream
And I love my music
Listening every week
My friends make me happy when I'm down
But really, don't make fun of my laugh
Well, that's all about me.

Isobel Cook (10)
Wakefield Methodist Junior & Infant School, Thornes

All About Me

Fiery hair as long as a rope.
Taurus is my star sign, horoscope.
My favourite thing to do is acting.
And I promise I am always practising.
Next September, cathedral is where I'm going.
And my talents for art will be showing.
I am the proud owner of eight little pets.
Five fish, a shrimp, a dog and my cat.
I am quite talented as you can see.
And that's my poem all about me.

Eliza Dorothy Hodgkins (10)
Wakefield Methodist Junior & Infant School, Thornes

This Is Me

You will need
A splash of horse riding
Make sure to add a drop of cucumber
A Fiat 500, only a pinch though
A handful of midwifery and a pinch of Norway
A gallon of kindness and a pound of intelligence.

Stir it all together, put it in the oven until you get a burst of orange
Then let it set and sprinkle a bit of bravery and a pinch of daftness
That's me to a tee!

Matilda Baker (10)
Wakefield Methodist Junior & Infant School, Thornes

How To Make Me

A litre of ginger and brown hair
A tablespoon of gaming
Add a sprinkle of fidgets
Don't forget to add sports
Add the Sagittarius sign
A tablespoon of songs
Mix it together and put it in the oven
Let it bake
When it turns purple it's ready
Sprinkle some outside playtime with my mates
And don't forget the loving time on top
And that's me!

Ava Mellor (10)
Wakefield Methodist Junior & Infant School, Thornes

This Is Me

My name is William
I have two dogs Pegy and George
I play on my Xbox with my best friends on Fortnite
My favourite subject is science
With booms and bangs
School is where I go to learn
When it's maths my mind gets lost
In the subtractions and times
When it's break time I'm energetic
I run around the field like a F1 car playing football.

William Barnsley (10)
Wakefield Methodist Junior & Infant School, Thornes

Recipe Of Me

Ingredients
A pinch of memes
A tablespoon of Nintendo Switch
A hint of messy but not the footballer
A scoop of kindness and happiness
A pinch of playing outside and with friends

Mix a pinch of memes and a pinch of playing outside
A scoop of kindness and a tablespoon of Switch
And throw in a hint of messiness
This is me!

Mac Copley (10)
Wakefield Methodist Junior & Infant School, Thornes

Me With A Double E

Believe it or not
I'm quite lonely
I don't have many friends
But the sacred ones I do have
Are perfect in every way
I am a definite dog person
I don't really like cats
I have a little brother and two mums
They're pretty great
My name is Ava Mae Dean Blades
And I'm amazing in all my ways.

Ava Mae Dean Blades (10)
Wakefield Methodist Junior & Infant School, Thornes

This Is Me

T otally busy so come tomorrow,
H ey, I like football, how about you?
I totally love YouTube,
S ometimes I play with my mates outside,

I like to play PS4,
S chool is boring when I'm not snoring,

M ashed peas and potatoes I hate,
E xactly this is me.

Mohammed Aslam (10)
Wakefield Methodist Junior & Infant School, Thornes

This Is Me

Ingredients:
A lot of McDonald's
A lot of sport
A pinch of TV
a spoon of my Xbox
A scoop of memes
A frying pan of school
A pinch of bravery

Mix:
Mix the Xbox and memes and put it in the oven
You get a spoon of school and a pinch of sports
And put them in the microwave
This is me.

Tommy Bramley (10)
Wakefield Methodist Junior & Infant School, Thornes

This Is Me

T etris is what I like
H arry Potter is my third favourite thing
I don't like mushrooms
S tampy is a YouTuber I like

I like Noah, he is my friend
S haun is my brother

M inecraft I love
E very day I watch the iPad.

C T Robinson-Rowe (10)
Wakefield Methodist Junior & Infant School, Thornes

This Is Me

A pinch of PS4,
One pound of striking,
Half a gram of chappati,
Fifteen grams of Celtic,
One-tenth of a gram of homework,
Seven grams of friends,
Two kilograms of Liverpool,
One pound of Ronaldo,

Stick it in the oven,
Add a dash of orange splash,
This is me!

Kasim Ramzan (10)
Wakefield Methodist Junior & Infant School, Thornes

What Makes Me Me

Why do I like strawberry milk?
Why am I blonde?
Why do I love the park?
Why am I not always right?
And why can't I fly like a kite?

The answer's a simple one, and that's really true,
The reason I'm like this is because this is me,
I'm not you.

Jessica Greer (10)
Wakefield Methodist Junior & Infant School, Thornes

Why

Oh, why did I fall off my bed when I was three?
And why did I break my toe when I was nine?
Oh, why do I build random Lego things to break them two days later?
The answer is simple you see,
To answer these and many more,
You must know these two words,
It's me!

Noah Christopher David Egan (10)
Wakefield Methodist Junior & Infant School, Thornes

All About Me

I'm curious
Sometimes I'm furious
I am clever
But I won't live forever
I am very silly
But my name isn't Billy
I'm not very bold
But I'm always told
To stop messing around
And not to make a sound.

Ali Sharif (10)
Wakefield Methodist Junior & Infant School, Thornes

This Is Me

As fast as Usain Bolt
I will try any food
My name is Dexter and I am nice
I love reading, I love eating
I will be nice if you be nice
I will play on my Xbox at any time
I watch movies
I know a lot of times tables.

Dexter Oakland (10)
Wakefield Methodist Junior & Infant School, Thornes

This Is Me

I look like a Japanese King
And I'm super smart
I like kickboxing
And I love art
I'm so kind
Though it doesn't make me tough
I want to be a doctor
If I work hard enough
This is me.

Nathan Williams (10)
Wakefield Methodist Junior & Infant School, Thornes

This Is Me

A pinch of PS5
Two and a half centimetres of fun
Two pinches of reading
One tube of family time
Two spoons of playing outside
Nine centimetres of carving wood
Mix it all
This is me!

Daud Rehman (10)
Wakefield Methodist Junior & Infant School, Thornes

This Is Me

I am
Ten
Fast
I train at football
I love oranges
I play with my friends on PS4
I'm a right-winger
And I play for Thornes Juniors
This is me.

Tien Tattersall (10)
Wakefield Methodist Junior & Infant School, Thornes

This Is Me

Things I like to do is watch YouTube and play games
I can be loving and caring
Sometimes I can be fun
I like to go outside
And can be very happy sometimes.

Dylan Smith (10)
Wakefield Methodist Junior & Infant School, Thornes

YoungWriters
Est. 1991

YOUNG WRITERS INFORMATION

We hope you have enjoyed reading this book – and that you will continue to in the coming years.

If you're the parent or family member of an enthusiastic poet or story writer, do visit our website **www.youngwriters.co.uk/subscribe** and sign up to receive news, competitions, writing challenges and tips, activities and much, much more! There's lots to keep budding writers motivated!

If you would like to order further copies of this book, or any of our other titles, then please give us a call or order via your online account.

Young Writers
Remus House
Coltsfoot Drive
Peterborough
PE2 9BF
(01733) 890066
info@youngwriters.co.uk

Join in the conversation!
Tips, news, giveaways and much more!

YoungWritersUK   **YoungWritersCW**   **youngwriterscw**